Entrepreneur Extraordinaire:
Grandpa Helps Emily Build a Business

By

J.M. Seymour

Illustrated by Will Hildebrandt

DynaMinds®
PUBLISHING

Entrepreneur Extraordinaire
Grandpa Helps Emily Build a Business

By J.M. Seymour

Illustrated by Will Hildebrandt
Book design by Creative Source

Thanks to the U.S. Small Business Administration,
Small Business Development Center, Iowa State University
Pappajohn Center for Entrepreneurship, other entrepreneurs,
and friends for help in preparing this book.

Printed in the United States of America

ISBN 9780971290020

Summary: Explains how to develop a business idea. The book is intended to provide an
understanding of the entrepreneurial process. Simple definitions explain basic business terms.

J.M. Seymour
Entrepreneur Extraordinaire: Grandpa Helps Emily Build a Business
  Business and economics—Juvenile literature.
  Entrepreneur—Juvenile literature.
  Financial education—Juvenile literature.

www.DynaMindsPublishing,com

"**I**'m sorry. We're out of cookies," said the clerk behind the counter.

"Again?" Emily was exasperated. This was the third day this week the convenience store was sold out when she stopped before soccer practice. Nothing else appealed like those chocolate chippers and juice.

"Can't you bake more?" she pleaded.

"Nope. We order as many as we can. They're just popular. You won't be the only one disappointed today," he replied.

Not really listening, Emily raced out, hoping her mom brought a snack for her sweet tooth later. Practice would be long enough without that cookie.

Emily was barely to the van when she spied her younger brother nibbling a muffin. She toppled her gear onto the floor, slipped inside, and tore open the white sack.

"And 'hi' to you, too, *Miss I'm Starving*," laughed Mom.

"Mmmmm...I *am* starving. I didn't get a cookie again," mumbled Emily between bites. "It's not fair. There are never enough."

"Well, why don't they order more cookies if demand is so great?" queried Mom.

"The owner said he tries, but can't. I think he needs a better supply...and a faster baker."

"Hmmm...**supply and demand**. Sounds like an entrepreneur's opportunity to me," her mom quipped.

"A what, Mom?" Emily asked.

6

What Is an Entrepreneur?

Someone starting a business often wears many hats. You might be the bookkeeper, office manager, salesperson, fundraiser, marketer, information technologist, president, secretary, and janitor.

And...you guessed it: The balancing act of doing everything—from making executive decisions, promoting, and selling products to budgeting, ordering supplies, and answering phones—can keep you busy. Once your business is up and running, you may hire expertise in some areas.

Take heart. Entrepreneurs under 30 start about one third of new businesses annually, according to estimates by the U.S. Small Business Administration.

Giving her young daughter a curious look, Mom explained. "When demand for something overtakes supply, someone usually sees a chance to make money. An **entrepreneur** is a person willing to take on the risk and fill the need. For example, your grandparents are entrepreneurs.

"America is filled with small businesses like theirs, well over 26.8, million, according to U.S. Small Business Administration estimates. Some small businesses are called micro-enterprises and home-based businesses, too. Your grandparents, like many others, see America as a land of great opportunity for an enterprising citizen who is willing to work."

"But Grandpa runs a boring car wash, and Grandma designs jewelry at home. How is that like making cookies?" Emily questioned her.

"Because an entrepreneur hopes to make money by supplying a needed service or product," replied her mom. "Your grandparents believe they can help make the world a better place."

"Can I be an entrepreneur then, too?" Emily asked, liking the idea of making money and remembering her grandparents' come-and-go lifestyle.

"Certainly," her mom replied. "Do you have an idea?"

Emily nodded. "Your cookies are as good as those at the convenience store, and the owner needs more. I've baked your cookies…it's not hard. I don't need a whole bakery, just your oven. Think of the money I could make.

The store charges $1.50 for a cookie. I could be rich!"
Emily imagined the possibilities, but Mom's skeptical look
was less than enthusiastic.

"Great idea, Emily, but starting a business takes work.
Let's see what Grandpa and Grandma say when they come
for dinner. You can make those cookies for dessert."

Her mind filled with ideas, Emily couldn't wait to announce her new business.

Her grandparents barely entered the front door before Emily peppered them with her ideas…"I'm starting a cookie business, Grandpa, and I'm going to be like you! I'll be rich!"

"Whoa…you what?!" Grandpa raised his eyebrows and chuckled.

Emily pulled him into the kitchen and poured out the details in bubbly fashion. Grandma listened and helped with dinner simultaneously.

"So…what do you think?" asked Emily as she took a breath.

Debbi Fields Lived The American Dream

In 1977, a 20-year-old mother with no business expertise wanted to open a cookie bakery in a California mall. Dismissing her idea as ludicrous, local bankers refused to loan her money. Businessmen ignored her product concept. Debbi Fields knew she baked a quality cookie, and was determined to start the business.

Fields finally opened her first store, and enticed customers by giving away warm, freshly baked cookies. Who could resist? Mrs. Fields Cookies became a multimillion-dollar company and the market leader among fresh-baked cookie stores. Mrs. Fields started franchises in 1990, and later sold her company.

Do not be afraid to take a chance, advises this entrepreneur.

To learn more about Mrs. Fields, read *One Smart Cookie: How a Housewife's Chocolate Chip Recipe Turned into a Multimillion-Dollar Business: The Story of Mrs. Fields Cookies* by Debbi Fields.

Forms of Ownership

How a business is structured affects taxation, vulnerability to lawsuits, and the owner's control. Forms of ownership could be:
- Sole proprietorship,
- Partnership,
- C Corporation,
- S Corporation or Subchapter S, and
- LLC or limited liability company.

Learn more about company structure at www.sba.gov.

Nodding, Grandpa shrugged, "It might be a great idea, and it might not, Em. Are you ready to figure out some things and then go to work? To make money, you must have a plan. Let me ask you some questions." Grandma winked at Grandpa and handed him some paper.

"First, will anyone buy your cookies?" asked Grandpa.

"Of course!" Emily retorted.

"Who?"

"Kids like me, " Emily explained. "Or maybe someone who stops for gas and wants a snack. Hey, everyone gets hungry. This shop has lots of food, but everyone loves a good, fresh cookie."

"But how do you know people will buy your cookies and not something else?" Grandpa continued.

Emily was a bit annoyed.

"Because the store sells out of cookies everyday, Grandpa, and the owner wishes he had more. He doesn't bake them himself, you know," replied Emily. "Mom's recipe is loads better, so my cookies would be popular. Besides, mine will be fresh and right by the cash register. Who wouldn't want a big, homemade, chocolate chip cookie for a snack? A cookie doesn't cost much. They sell for $1.50 now. And, the owner will buy my cookies, because he likes me and sees me in there, usually with friends. I *know* how a good cookie should taste!"

One Small Idea Launches...a Google

It was 1998, the height of the "Dotcom" era.

Two PhD students at Stanford University—Larry Page and Sergey Brin—had an idea to license Internet search engine technology. They maxed out their credit cards to buy a terabyte of memory and built their own computer network in Larry's dorm room, the company's first data center.

Page and Brin wrongly assumed a company would buy their idea. But true to entrepreneurial form, they launched it themselves when no company showed interest. To raise capital, they wrote a business plan and sought investors. A faculty member led them to Andy Bechtolsheim, a founder of Sun Microsystems. He wrote a check for $100,000 and helped them start Google, Inc.

Page and Brin never looked back. Google garnered more venture capital, gained media attention, and added many employees. The first year, their search engine answered more than 500,000 queries a day. Innovative search technology transformed their college research project into a major public corporation and made them rich.

Grandpa grinned and patted her on the back. "For just concocting this idea, Em, you are doing a great job thinking and sorting out business details. Actually, you are forming a simple **business plan**."

"I am?" Emily looked puzzled.

Grandpa held out his paper. "Look at this. Here is what you told me about your potential business. "

Type of business: food manufacturing

✓ Product: Chocolate chip cookies

✓ Package: Sold individually

✓ Point of sale: Convenience store, at checkout counter

✓ Product benefits:
- Fresh, homemade from a tested recipe
- Jumbo Size
- Cheap Snack
- Tasty
- Popular with kids

✓ Customer: Convenience shop that already sells food to hungry kids

✓ Competition: Other cookies, similar snack foods sold in the store

Sales force: Emily

✓ Supplier: Current baker can't keep up with demand for cookies

Price: $1.50

Labor: Emily

How Does a Business Get Started?

Idea for product (or service)....Discuss with others...Write a business plan...

Product prototype... Protect the idea

Market research...Test product in markets...Refine design

Set a price ...Develop a brand

Find suppliers...

Market and sell...Tally profit/loss...

Product update...Revisit price...New product...

What Is a Business Plan and Why Do I Need It?

An entrepreneur's vision can sound great, but will the idea make money? To see if your idea makes sense, write a good business plan. This is a detailed, working document that can:

- Uncover potential problems,
- Provide strategic direction , and
- Forecast profits and/or losses.

Vital to business success, a business plan should include:

- Executive overview or summary,
- Company description,
- Products or services description,
- Organization structure,
- Market analysis,
- Sales strategy,
- Marketing strategy,
- Funding needs, and
- Financial picture and forecast.

For business plan basics, see the Appendix.

Excellent resources exist for writing business plans. Start with the U.S. Small Business Administration website at www.sba.gov or the affiliated Small Business Development Centers at www.asbdc-us.org.

"Many entrepreneurs come up with great ideas, but they forget to plan to succeed at business. If you can't make money, even a fantastic idea is not a smart *venture*. Let's see how you will make money with your cookie business," Grandpa suggested.

"That's easy," replied Emily. "The store owner will pay me when I deliver."

"It may not be as simple as that, Em. You just told me you will be the cookie *manufacturer* who sells to a *retailer* and not directly to the end user, or final customer, right?"

"But if the store owner sells my cookies, I get the money. What's the difference if I'm the manufacturer or retailer, Grandpa?"

"Price, packaging, and promotion, to name a few. First, let's take a look at price. You want to make a *profit*, but your buyer wants to make money when he *resells* cookies, too. So he cannot pay your full price per cookie. You will have to *discount* your product, so he can *mark-up* his merchandise. Does that make sense?"

Emily wrinkled her nose. Grandpa just cut into her expected profits.

Name Your Business

Finding a business name is more complex than just dreaming up something clever.

1) Give thought to legalities. Must you include "Inc." for a **corporation** or "LLC" for a **partnership**?

2) Try to create a one-of-a-kind **trade name**. Using your own name is one of the easier ways to have a unique business name. Example: *Emily's Great Gourmet Cookies.*

3) Make your business name easy to remember and easy to pronounce.

4) Stay away from confusing words or names already associated with another company. Business names can be registered through your state's Secretary of State office and the U.S. Patent and Trademark Office. Start your own search at www.uspto.gov/web/trademarks/workflow/start.htm and a search engine such as www.google.com.

5) Should your business name be the same as your **domain name** for a website and on-line sales? Domain names, while not registered with the government, can be found and purchased from www.HostMySite.com, www.google.com or other on-line sources. Most will let you know if the domain name is already taken.

6) Think about descriptive words for your industry. Do some have negative connotations or limit your scope of business? Use www.wordlab.com/tools/t_index.cfm as a starting point.

Make It Legal

Food products are regulated, so check legal requirements when manufacturing.

- Are separate kitchen facilities required?
- Do you need a license to handle food products and raw materials?
- Must you meet certain criteria to produce from a home location or to sell directly to consumers?
- Does your product label meet requirements?
- Are periodic government inspections required?
- Can you meet food safety and sanitation regulations?

Other businesses might require special permits or have zoning restrictions, too. Be sure to obey laws in your community.

"Now, when the retailer sells your cookies, you should also expect to make money and be happy, right?" Grandpa continued.

Emily nodded with more enthusiasm.

"That means your price must include ample profit or you don't do it, no matter how much you love the idea. So...to price cookies, you need to consider what customers like your friends—the end users—will pay, what the retailer is willing to pay you, and what the product costs you to produce." Grandpa wrote a formula:

Price to retailer – cost to produce = Emily's profit

"Now, let's work on production costs. We should include raw **_materials, labor, packaging, promotion,_** and **_overhead_**."

"What's overhead, Grandpa?" Emily interrupted.

"Overhead includes items you need to make the product, whether you produce one batch or 1,000 batches. In your cookie baking, overhead means baking pans and utensils, oven and refrigerator, electricity, water, clean-up supplies, and extras such as a phone, office supplies, and transportation to get ingredients and make deliveries."

"But mom has all that already. Can't I just use her kitchen and have her drive me?" Emily looked confused.

"Yes, and maybe your mother won't pass along the costs," Grandpa agreed. "But you should still consider overhead an expense, no matter who pays those bills."

What Business Will You Start?

Businesses, like people, come in many shapes and sizes. To find one best suited to you:

1) Think about what you do everyday. Do you want to be outside? Is working by yourself okay? Do you like doing tasks for others? Like pets? Like to handle money and use a cash register? Like to work certain hours of the day? Like to sell things? Or would you rather make things?

2) Think about your skills. Are you easily motivated? Organized? Creative?

3) Consider jobs that fit you. Here are some ideas young entrepreneurs try:
- Dog groomer
- Babysitter
- House sitter
- Gardener
- Swimming lesson teacher
- Cookie baker
- Garage sale organizer
- Lawn mower
- Farmers' market stand owner

Who Is Your Customer?

Some entrepreneurs sell products to an **end user** (the final consumer) and some to a **middleman** (reseller). Packaging, advertising, and marketing strategies vary, depending on whether the product is delivered in bulk or individually packaged.

Wholesalers produce and sell to another business that uses the product in manufacturing. Examples: Farmers supply corn to General Mills (manufacturer) and to grocery stores (retailer); Ykk® sells zippers to Levi Strauss (manufacturer) and to fabric stores (retailer).

Manufacturers mass produce a product using raw materials purchased from suppliers. Examples: Ford makes autos with a variety of parts, Kraft makes frozen pizzas by combining several ingredients.

Retailers buy finished products for resale. Sears buys Levis® jeans and Goodyear® tires to sell to individual consumers.

Service businesses perform a chore for consumers. Examples: Florist, restaurant, drycleaner, tailor, consultant.

Could Emily's cookie business fall under more than one category? Over time, could she change her customer base?

Grandpa continued. "Now, let's consider raw materials, which might be your major expense. What will you need, Em?"

"That's easy," replied Emily. "Lots of eggs, sugar, flour, butter, chocolate chips, and… everything else on Mom's recipe."

"Good," Grandpa nodded. "How will you get these raw materials? Will you buy in large quantity—**bulk purchases**? Or, will you buy just enough for one batch at a time—a **just-in-time inventory**? How you buy affects profits. Plus, your price to the retailer must remain about the same each delivery, or he won't know how to set a price for his customers."

"Hmmm," Emily thought she might do both. "It depends how many cookies I'm making a day, how long the ingredients stay fresh, and if I find some ingredients on sale. More grocery store trips mean more overhead, but rotten eggs would stink," Emily laughed.

Price for Profit

Setting your product's price may seem easy…a no-brainer.
- Will your market accept your price?
- How are competing products priced?
- Can **production costs** vary from day to day, season to season?
- Will **inventory** get old, lose value, be discarded or sold at discount?
- Must a middleman be paid or will you sell direct?
- Does your market change quickly, always looking for the next new thing?

To keep the optimum **profit margin** for your business, know production costs, keep **overhead expenses** in line, and buy the **raw materials** when prices are best.

There are two ways to make more **profit**:
- **Increase income**
- **Reduce expenses**

For example, Emily can probably make cookies for less if she gets a lower price by buying more raw materials (eggs, flour). But if she can't use the extra and has no place to store inventory, ingredients would be wasted. And, she could buy cheaper ingredients (shortening instead of butter) but her product quality may suffer.

Do Small and Home-Based Businesses Pay Taxes?

If your new business makes a profit, expect to pay:

- Federal income tax and
- State and/or local income tax.

You might also pay:

- Sales tax from customers (reported and sent to state treasurer),
- Sales tax (when you buy goods to use),
- Federal and state unemployment taxes (if you have employees),
- Workers compensation tax (if you have employees), and
- Social Security payroll taxes (again, with employees).

"Good thinking, Em," Grandpa chuckled too. "Now, what about labor?"

"Labor?"

"Yes, who will make cookies?" Grandpa asked.

"I can make them myself, and I won't need Mom's help, thank you!" Emily gave Grandpa another indignant look.

"Not so fast," Grandpa added. "I didn't mean you weren't capable of baking, Em. I look ahead to when you might have more orders than one person can handle, or you are busy with soccer tournaments and can't be baking. Will you get extra help or will you just produce limited quantities?"

"Gee, I hadn't thought about it. That's probably why the store owner can't get more cookies from his other baker, right?"

"Exactly. Down the road, you might hire help to produce larger *volume*. While this can mean less profit per cookie, you might see more total profit by expanding quantities efficiently. Of course, your own time is worth something too. Either way, consider labor an expense," Grandpa said.

"Now, let's think about packaging and promotion," Grandpa said. "What is needed to protect the cookies from damage, and how must they be packaged for sale to the eventual consumer?"

"I don't have a clue," Emily grimaced and smacked her forehead. "The store owner sells cookies from a tray, and just hands me one. I don't think I care about a package, do I?"

"Okay, your competition uses no packaging," Grandpa acknowledged. "Can you think of an easy solution to make your cookies look more appealing, so buyers want yours instead?"

Emily shrugged her shoulders and shook her head.

"How about clear plastic wrap to keep cookies fresher and a hot pink sticker that says, *Emily's Best Cookies*? Customers might buy extra if cookies are packaged 'to go'."

"It sounds awesome but expensive, Grandpa."

"That depends," Grandpa replied. "If it's true the storeowner sells his entire supply of cookies every day, you may not need to promote your **brand** much. But what if you need to get noticed, so your cookies sell before the competition? Then you must be different. In your case, several day-old cookies every day means no profit. But, if you can keep your cookies fresh longer, you may not need to bake as often. That might save labor costs, too. With a little **market research**, we could see if packaging and promotion are needed or not, Em."

Build a Great Brand

Customers and potential customers should easily recognize and find your products. That's why you will want to build a brand. How?

1) Create a logo, or graphic symbol, to represent your business. It should be:
   - Unique and unlike a competitor's logo,
   - A simple, eye-catching design,
   - Easy to reproduce, and
   - A look that relates to your business.

2) Use your logo often – on business cards, letterhead, advertising, t-shirts, product packaging, website, and more.

3) Develop an easy-to-remember slogan (a sentence or phrase) to accompany your logo. This helps you describe the product in a fun, attractive way when someone asks, "What's your business?".

"What is market research?"

"Oh, it just means we scout the competition, find out about customers who buy cookies, discover the sales potential for your cookies, and learn how to set the best price," Grandpa explained simply. "Market research might mean we do a customer survey, study a competitor's **business model**,

give out samples, or ask store owners a few questions. We're trying to find the best way to sell and make a profit with the least amount of work.

"You may have to give away some sample cookies. Is that okay?" He asked.

Emily shrugged. "I guess."

"You might also give coupons for free cookies to drive traffic to the store. It will help build a **customer base**, especially in the beginning. Maybe the owner would cooperate with you on **advertising** like that, because visitors would also buy other items. What if you gave out coupons at soccer tournaments?"

Emily liked that idea. "Yeah, that would be great. But why do I care? Everyone will like these cookies, Grandpa!"

Grandpa shook his head.

"You know, Em, many entrepreneurs think everyone wants their products," he acknowledged. "But that's really a mistake. While it sounds logical since most everyone enjoys cookies at some time, that doesn't translate into automatic sales. For some buyers, price might be a barrier to a purchase. For others, flavor or taste might stop them. For others, it might be a timing issue. Getting and keeping customers is a challenge for any entrepreneur or business," Grandpa said.

"Once you find a formula that works, stick with it. **Repeat customers** make for efficient—and profitable—business. It's easier to advertise and sell to a **niche market** than to everyone anyway."

"Niche market?" Her curiosity piqued.

"Yes. That means you focus energy on selling to a select group with potential to be your best customers and bring repeat business. Another name is

target market, because you are aiming for the bull's-eye," Grandpa explained. "Most entrepreneurs find this more profitable than chasing the universe of *everyone.*"

"Oh, once customers taste my cookies, they'll come back for more. But I didn't think making money would take this much work," Emily mused. "I thought the hard work was making cookies!"

27

"Still want to try?"
Grandpa asked.

"Why not?" Emily shrugged.
"What's to lose?"

"I like your attitude, Em,"
he chuckled.

"Successful entrepreneurs aren't afraid to dive in and take *calculated risks*. Many great companies are born after an entrepreneur started an idea in a garage, basement, or kitchen. In fact, companies like Microsoft, Dell, Google, Hershey, and

Promoting Your Biz?
Create a Buzz

Get customers to buy your product by smart marketing—create a promotional buzz.

Here are some ideas to announce your new business:

- Send a press release to media
- Distribute flyers
- Hang door hangers in neighborhoods
- Give out discount coupons
- Mail postcards to friends and relatives
- Get featured in newspaper stories
- Buy advertising
- Give out samples
- Create a website or blog
- Donate products for a fundraiser
- Print and use business cards
- Put posters on store bulletin boards

Protect Your Product

Protect your product through the U.S. Patent and Trademark Office in Washington D.C.

1) If you create a product (or service) with a unique name and logo, apply for a registered **trademark**. The ® can be displayed after approval, but ™ can be used if you have applied. Examples are Kleenex® tissue, Dasani® bottled water, or Panera® bread.

2) A **copyright** protects original, written creations, such as books, videos, plays, cartoons, artwork, and music. The © can be displayed immediately.

3) Apply for a **patent** if you invent a process, a product with moving parts, or have a recipe to produce it. Products using several unique technologies may require several patents. Each of these applications takes time and costs money. Keep in mind the "idea" itself cannot be protected. It's your unique product (or prototype) which can earn the protection.

Kellogg's began that way. That's what makes America's *free enterprise* system so great. Anyone with an idea and the motivation to execute it can launch a business. Work hard and, with a little luck, you can be a success. It doesn't matter whether you are young or old, male or female, if you just moved to America, or if you have a college degree. What matters most is minding your business."

"Minding my business, Grandpa?" Emily looked curious.

"Yes, Em. Good business owners pay attention to key factors. We've really already talked about them." Grandpa ticked off five points on his right hand. "You want to:

1) *Plan* to succeed...because that's the most important part of running a business.

2) Start with a *niche market*...because *everybody* is not a good target.

3) *Fill a need* with a product (or service)...make it unique and good quality.

4) Find great *customers*...and keep them happy for repeat business.

5) Manage for *profit*...and learn to be a good recordkeeper."

"Got it," Emily nodded and grinned. "But I still think everyone will buy my cookies."

"I hope they do, Em!" Grandpa laughed and turned his head toward the counter. "Shall we do a taste test and see how much I am willing to pay?" And he reached for the warm cookies.

Appendix
Anatomy of a Business Plan

A good business plan includes:

- Executive overview or summary,
- Company description,
- Products or services,
- Market analysis,
- Organization structure,

- Sales strategy,
- Marketing strategy,
- Funding needs, and
- Financial picture.

1

Executive Overview
This one-page summary includes the mission statement, founders' names, location, list of products/services, birds' eye view of expected company growth, summary of future plans.

2

Company Description
Describe how the elements of your business fit together.
   A) Include reasons why you are starting a business in this industry as well as a list of key factors that should make your business a success.
   B) List the customer needs you strive to fulfill, including how your product(s) will satisfy them. What is your competitive advantage?
   C) Finally, list specific individuals and/or organizations having these needs – your markets.

Service or Product Line
Describe your product(s) or service(s), and highlight benefits you provide customers.
   • How does your service or product provide a solution to a problem?
   • What is your competitive advantage?

Can you show how potential customers are willing to pay for the solution you can provide? Give details about suppliers, availability, and costs. Give details about new products you may add in the future.

4

Market Analysis
This section details how your product/service will impact the industry. Include target markets, research on competitors, market research data, and a description of your industry.
If you have done any test marketing, include summaries.

5

Organization and Management
Include your company's organizational structure and details about ownership. Describe each division/department and its function. Give profiles of your management team and board of directors, including their backgrounds and reasons you want them as board members or employees. Describe salary and benefits packages you have (or plan to have). How will you handle promotions, bonuses, or incentives?

6 Marketing and Sales

The process of creating and selling customers is your marketing and sales strategy.
First, define your *marketing strategy*. This plan would include:
- Market penetration,
- Plan for growing your business,
- Channels of distribution, and
- Communication plan.

Overall *sales strategy* includes:
- Sales force plans and
- Sales activities.

7 Funding Requests

If you are using your business plan to find funding, you should include in this section:
- Current funding requirement,
- Future funding requirements for the next five years,
- How you plan to use the funds, and
- Long-range financial strategies that would impact your funding request.

8 Financials

You can allocate resources most efficiently if you develop financials after you analyze the market and set objectives.
- How much money do you need to begin?
- How much of your own money can you afford to invest?
- Where can you find this investment equity, or money? (Savings, gift from Grandpa, loan from mom?)

Your business plan should include:
- Annual income statements, balance sheets, and cash flow statements for up to 3 to 5 years of business operation;
- Future forecast of income and cash flow;
- Collateral you could use to ensure your loan, should you want one, and
- Short analysis of financial statements. (Graphs work well to show trends.)

Glossary

Accountant . . . . The person who measures, records, and communicates the financial information for a company.

Accounts payable . . . . Liabilities, or money owed by an individual or company.

Accounts receivable . . . . Money owed to your company—outstanding bills.

Acquisition . . . . A company may agree to buy another company, providing the shareholders of the merged company with cash or securities for their shares.

Advertising . . . . The art of communicating a company or product's features via print publications, billboards, television, radio, websites, trinkets, direct mail, or other media. Advertising is paid promotion.

APR . . . . Annual percentage rate; the interest on a loan for one year, whether the loan is for longer or shorter than 12 months. Use this rate to compare two loans.

Assets . . . . Something of value that is owned, such as inventory or equipment. Assets are listed on the balance sheet.

Balance sheet . . . . A financial statement that shows what the company owns (assets), what the company owes (liabilities), and what the owner's value (equity) equals at one point in time.

Bankruptcy . . . . Individuals or businesses having more debts than assets can file legal paperwork to process through issues and liquidate assets, according to federal law.

Board of Directors . . . . This group of individuals represent the shareholders of a corporation. The board holds meetings, as set by the corporation by-laws. Each board member represents one vote. The board is responsible for assessing the company management (the people) and business activity.

B2B (business to business) . . . . One company sells to another company and not the end consumer.

Boom . . . . A robust economic period where companies thrive, demand of goods and services increases.

Boom-bust cycle . . . . A total economic cycle encompassing both the high (boom) to low (bust).

Brand . . . . A logo—identifying symbol or mark—to make your product or company unique, different from competitors.

Break-even point . . . . When sales are equal to fixed expenses plus variable costs, the break-even point has been reached and then profit begins.

Budget . . . . A proposal that estimates the amount of money spent and received for a certain time period, such as a year.

Buy in bulk . . . . Purchase of large quantities, generally at a discounted price.

Business plan . . . . A set of working documents that include a description of the business, customer profile, marketing and sales strategies, sources for materials and labor, start-up costs, and financial information, which can be used for a profit-and-loss statement, balance sheet, and analyzing the breakeven point.

Business model . . . . An example of a good company and how it runs.

Bust . . . . An economic period of recession where demand of goods and services decreases.

Calculated risk . . . . Variability that is based on information or facts that appear to reduce the overall uncertainty.

C Corp . . . . An incorporated business—a legal, taxable entity—having shareholders.

Capital . . . . The money provided to finance a company. It can be from common stock, bonds, venture capital, loans, profits from the business.

Cash flow . . . . The difference between cash received and cash spent.

CEO . . . . Chief executive officer; the person who oversees the entire company, usually a corporation.

CFO . . . . Chief financial officer; the person handling a company's financial aspects.

Collateral . . . . A tangible asset offered as security for a loan.

Commission . . . . A salesperson's fee for the amount of business brought in.

Competition. . . . . Two or more individuals or companies vie for the business of a customer or group of customers.

Consumer. A buyer of a product or service.

Copyright. A right granted by the U.S. government to protect a creator's literary or artistic work.

Corporation. . . . . A taxable, legal entity recognized by state or federal government as a business owned by shareholders.

Cost of Goods Sold (COGS) . . . . What is paid to buy and transform raw materials into a product for sale, usually for one accounting period (such as one fiscal year). COGS can include labor, overhead, and depreciation as well as raw materials.

Credit . . . . Accounting term that means subtract, or decrease the asset column.

Customer . . . . A buyer of a product or services.

Debit . . . . Accounting term that means add, or increase the asset column.

Debt . . . . Another name for liability, or an obligation to pay. Debt is listed under liabilities on the balance sheet.

Demographics . . . . Sorting population according to characteristics, such as age, income, gender, residence, education level.

Depreciation . . . . When a tangible asset is used up during the business, the business deducts the value of that asset over its entire life rather than as a one-time expense. For example, a $600 oven might be listed as a $600 asset in year one, $550 asset in year two, $500 asset in year three, and so on. So the oven depreciates about $50 per year, which is the oven's annual cost figured in the production of cookies.

Discount. . . . . A reduced price offered for a product or service.

Distribution. . . . . Movement of goods from one point to another.

Distributor. . . . . An individual or company that moves products or raw materials from manufacturer to customer.

Diversification. . . . . Expanding investments or product lines over a broad or diverse area.

Dividends . . . . Income a company pays shareholders on a regular basis (monthly, annually, but generally quarterly), usually expressed as dividend per share.

E Commerce . . . . Business conducted by Internet website.

Employee . . . . Workers paid on behalf of a company or business.

Entrepreneur . . . . Someone who sees opportunity or is interested in taking a business risk in return for profitable reward.

Equity . . . . The amount of money contributed by the owner(s) to start a business. For example, a baker who started a cookie business by buying $100 in utensils and pans would have $100 equity in the business.

Expenses . . . . Items paid for and deducted as costs to a business; opposite of income.

Fiscal year . . . . 12-month period a company uses to compute profit and losses. It may not necessarily line up with the calendar year.

Fixed cost . . . . Expense that remains unchanged, no matter how many units are manufactured. For example: Cookies can be delivered to a store for $10 per trip. It does not matter if 20 or 200 cookies are delivered to the store, because the same delivery charge is incurred.

Franchise . . . . A licensing arrangement that allows an individual to sell a branded product or service in return for paying a fee.

Free enterprise . . . . A business environment where companies can operate without excessive government controls.

Goods . . . . Another name for products manufactured.

Gross profit . . . . Total revenue minus the cost of goods sold.

Gross sales . . . . Total dollars taken in for products or services sold, not adjusted for customer returns. It is calculated by adding all invoices and receipts.

Income . . . . Revenue minus expenses.

Income tax . . . . A fee levied against net profit of a business or company.

Income statement	This shows revenues received and expenses paid by a business over a certain time period, usually annually or quarterly.
Inflation	An economic period where prices for goods and services rise; opposite of recession.
Insurance	Protection against a catastrophe, provided for a fee.
IRS	Internal Revenue Service; branch of the U.S. government that collects taxes.
Inventory	A tally of the raw materials and the resulting products being manufactured and later sold. For example, flour, eggs, and chocolate chips would be inventory items for a cookie business, and so would the baked cookies.
Invoice	A request, or bill, for payment for goods or services sold. A business would send a customer such a request for payment.
K-1	A business provides this IRS form to sharerholders who need to report a profit or loss from the business on their individual tax return.
Labor	Work—or workers—needed to produce a product.
Liabilities	Also called debt, or obligation to pay. Liabilities are listed on the balance sheet.
Limited liability corporation	A business structure acting similar to a partnership but taxed as a corporation. Often referred to as LLC.
Logo	An image or graphic mark that identifies a product or company.
Loss	Having more expenses than sales, results in a negative amount. Opposite of profit.
Manufacturer	An individual or company that produces a product from raw materials.
Mark-up	The difference between cost of making the product and selling price of the product.
Market	The intended consumers (individuals and businesses) that have a need or desire for your product.

38

Marketing . . . . The process of using advertising, sales, research, and public relations strategies to create a sale. It has been summed up as 4 Ps: product, place, pricing, promotion.

Market research . . . . A process that provides insights to understand more about customers, competitors, and factors that affect business, sales, and product development.

Merger . . . . Two companies combine to form one.

Net profit . . . . Revenue minus expenses.

Net sales . . . . Total dollars received after all costs associated with the product are deducted. Gross sales minus customer returns and allowances for damaged goods equals net sales.

Net worth . . . . Also called owner or shareholder equity. On a balance sheet, a business lists assets (inventory plus cash on hand) minus liabilities (debt) to equal net worth or equity.

Niche market . . . . A targeted, small portion of a population. A small businessperson often focuses on serving a target group with similar demographics.

Overhead . . . . An expense not tied to one product but rather an overall cost of doing business, such as rent, commissions, computer hardware.

Packaging . . . . Product wrapper to get it marketed, distributed, and sold in optimum condition.

Partnership . . . . A form of ownership, where two or more individuals run a business together, sharing both the profits and losses and paying their own share of income taxes.

Patent . . . . The U.S. government issues this protection to someone who invents a product or process.

Profit . . . . The amount left after expenses are paid; also called net income. Earnings minus expenses equals profit.

Profit and loss statement . . . . Also called income and expense statement. This shows how cash flows for a business and summarizes revenues and expenses for one time period, such as a month or year.

Profit margin . . . . Measures profits as percent of revenue.

Promotion . . . . Strategies a business uses to show a target market the value of its products.

Quality control . . . . Process to ensure a business' products or services are consistent.

Raw materials . . . . Goods needed to manufacture a new product. Raw materials appear as an inventory item on the asset side of a balance sheet.

Receipt . . . . Individual record proving that goods or services were exchanged. A business would provide a customer such a record to show proof of the amount paid.

Recession . . . . An economic period where prices of goods and services is not rising quickly; opposite of inflation.

Reconcile . . . . Process of matching and comparing your financial records against another source, such as the bank's monthly statement of your account.

Repeat customers . . . . Those who buy a company's products more than once.

Resale, resell . . . . When a product manufacturer sells to a retail business owner—who pays a discounted price and intends to sell that product to an end consumer for a higher price—then the product is for "resale." With products for resale, the retailer, not the manufacturer , generally reports any sales tax incurred.

Retailer . . . . A business that sells one or more products to the consumer.

Return on investment . . . . Also called return on assets and refers to how much income can be earned from assets in a given period. To calculate return on investment, divide net profits by total assets.

Revenue . . . . Money received for sales of goods or services. Revenue can include product sales, cash receipts from rental payments, and interest.

Salary . . . . Another name for wages paid; cost of the labor needed to manufacture a product or do business.

Sales . . . . Cash receipts from sale of products or services.

Sales forecast . . . . Prediction of cash receipts for sale of products or services, generally for a particular fiscal period.

Schedule C . . . . Sole proprietors or unincorporated business owners file this IRS form annually to report a profit or loss.

Selling price . . . . The amount a customer pays to receive goods or services from a business.

Service . . . . The expertise or labor a business offers for sale. For example, a window washer is paid for providing labor rather than an actual product.

Service mark . . . . A way to protect the uniqueness of a brand, via the U.S. government.

Shareholder . . . . Owner of one or more shares of stock in a corporation.

Sole proprietor . . . . An individual who owns and operates an unincorporated small business.

Start-Up costs . . . . The amount of money needed to begin product manufacture, but limited to items that will be reused and not consumed. Start-up costs do not include cost of goods sold. For example, a cookie business could include baking sheets, mixing bowls, and measuring spoons in start-up costs. But flour, eggs, and chips are raw materials, or cost of goods sold.

Subchapter S Corporation . . . . An incorporated business where the owners choose to
(or Sub S) be taxed as a partnership.

Subcontractor . . . . One who agrees to perform work or produce a product for another business.

Supplier . . . . An individual or business that provides raw materials or services for another business.

Supply and demand . . . . A way of describing the economics between buyers and sellers of products or services, where price and quantity of product sold are determined by the wants /needs of buyers and the production output of sellers.

Target audience . . . . Intended consumers of your product. A business may choose to market and sell to one or several target audiences.

Trademark . . . . A unique logo, symbol, design or image that identifies a product or service and its source. Trademarks protect intellectual property and are granted by the U.S. Patent and Trademark Office.

Variable cost . . . . Also called overhead or indirect costs. These costs change, or vary, depending upon how many product units are manufactured. For example: One baker can produce 100 cookies per hour, but two bakers are needed to produce 200 cookies per hour. Labor is a variable cost.

Venture . . . . A major undertaking or strategic alliance, similar to an adventure. Venture can refer to a joint venture (agreement between two business parties) or venture capital (financial help).

Venture capitalist . . . . An individual or organization that provides equity, or financing, for an entrepreneur, who may have a business idea deemed too risky for a bank to grant a large loan.

Wages . . . . Another name for salary, or payments for work done. Cost of the labor needed to manufacture product.

Order Form

Please send *Entrepreneur Extraordinaire: Grandpa Helps Emily Build a Business* to the following.

I enclosed $20.00 per book (free shipping). TOTAL enclosed: $_____

Name _____

Address _____

City_____

State, ZIP _____

Email _____

Name _____

Address _____

City_____

State, ZIP _____

Email _____

Name _____

Address _____

City_____

State, ZIP _____

Email _____

Please make check payable to DynaMinds Publishing, 6119 Nottingham, Johnston, IA 50131;
email Chuck@DynaMindsPublishing.com

About the author

J.M. Seymour is an entrepreneur, financial educator and journalist. She founded a marketing communications company four years after graduating from Iowa State University, and is the author of several children's books, including the award-winning *Stock Market Pie: Grandma Helps Emily Make a Million and What's Your Money Personality* booklet. Also known as The Money Godmother®, Ms. Seymour speaks and blogs to youth, parents, and others about ideas to manage money and create wealth.

She has served as Iowa's chair for Money Smart Week, as president for the Iowa Jump$tart Coalition, and as a board member for several foundations and community organizations. She is a founding member of the Iowa Enterprise Network and The Center for Financial Success, and has been nationally recognized as SBA's Midwest region Home-Based Business Advocate of the Year.

Ms. Seymour and her husband reside near Des Moines, IA, where they together run two businesses.

About the illustrator

Will Hildbrandt is an artist and art teacher living in LeGrand, IA. He has been a professional student of the arts for more than 30 years. Will received his BA in art/art education from Wartburg College and his Master of Arts in studio art/drawing from the University of Northern Iowa.